Amazing Animals
Sheep

Please visit our Web site, www.garethstevens.com. For a free color catalog of all our high-quality books, call toll free 1-800-542-2595 or fax 1-877-542-2596.

Library of Congress Cataloging-in-Publication Data

Wilsdon, Christina.
  Sheep / Christina Wilsdon.
    p. cm. — (Amazing animals)
  Includes index.
  ISBN 978-1-4339-4029-3 (pbk.)
  ISBN 978-1-4339-4030-9 (6 pack)
  ISBN 978-1-4339-4028-6 (library binding)
  1. Sheep—Juvenile literature. I. Title.
  SF375.2.W55 2010
  636.3—dc22
                          2010016547

This edition first published in 2011 by
Gareth Stevens Publishing
111 East 14th Street, Suite 349
New York, NY 10003

Editor: Greg Roza
Designer: Christopher Logan

Photo credits: Cover, back cover, pp. 1, 3, 4–5, 6–7, 8–9, 10–11, 12–13, 13 (bottom), 14–15, 16–17, 17 (inset), 18–19, 20–21, 22–23, 24–25, 25 (inset), 26–27, 28–29, 30–31, 32–33, 34 (left), 34–35, 36–37, 38–39, 40 (inset), 40–41, 44–45, 46 Shutterstock.com/Derek Abbott; pp. 10 (bottom), 18 (bottom) © Nova Development Corp.; p. 9 (bottom) © Dreamstime.com/Derek Abbott; pp. 10 (bottom), 18 (bottom) © Nova Development Corp.; p. 29 (bottom) © iStockphoto.com/Andraz Cerar; p. 33 (bottom) © iStockphoto.com/Lawrence Sawyer; pp. 42–43 © iStockphoto.com/Jeremy Voisey.

Printed in the United States of America

CPSIA compliance information: Batch #CS10GS: For further information contact Gareth Stevens, New York, New York at 1-800-542-2595.

Amazing Animals
Sheep

By Christina Wilsdon

Contents

Chapter 1
A Sheep Story

Wild Words

A male sheep is called a ram. A female sheep is called a ewe (YOO). A young sheep is called a lamb.

A fluffy flock of sheep moved slowly across the field of the small farm. Every sheep was busy eating grass. Every sheep, that is, except Mama Sheep. She was too restless to eat. She knew her baby would be born soon.

Mama Sheep wandered back to the barn and found a stall full of straw. She dug a little nest and lay down in it. A few hours later, Baby Sheep arrived. He lay in the straw while Mama Sheep licked him from head to toe.

"Baa, baa," she murmured as she scrubbed him clean. She nudged him with her nose. The little lamb stood up and took his first wobbly steps. Mama Sheep **nuzzled** him as he drank his first meal of milk.

Spotted Sheep

Jacob sheep have a wool coat that's white with black spots. The black wool grows a bit longer than the white wool.

9

For a few days, Mama Sheep and Baby Sheep stayed together in the stall. The farmer kept the other sheep away from them so Mama could take good care of her baby.

"Baaaa!" said Baby Sheep in a high-pitched voice. Mama Sheep replied with a long, deep "Baaaa!" Baby Sheep knew the sound of Mama Sheep's bleat, just as she knew his. Knowing the sound of each other's voice would help them find each other in the flock.

Mama Sheep had raised a few sets of twins over the years. This was the first time she had given birth to just one baby. But caring for even one lamb was hard work!

The Tail's End

Why do many sheep have short tails? Farmers often remove part of a lamb's tail soon after birth. This is called docking. Tails are docked to help keep sheep clean and stop flies from bothering them.

Wild Words

The sound a sheep makes, *baa*, is called a bleat.

Sometimes when lambs play together, they practice skills they need later in life, such as head butting.

After a few days, Mama Sheep and Baby Sheep joined a group of ewes and lambs. Baby Sheep stuck close to his mother. Mama Sheep angrily butted any other lambs that came too close to him. Baby Sheep quickly discovered that other lambs were fun playmates. The lambs ran and skipped. They butted heads. When Baby Sheep was tired or hungry, he scampered back to Mama Sheep.

Baby Sheep mostly ate Mama Sheep's milk. He also ate feed that the farmer put out just for the lambs. The farmer put the feed into a stall that was just the right size for the lambs to creep into, but too small for the ewes to enter.

Baby Sheep grew quickly. He weighed about 6 pounds (2.7 kg) when he was born. By the time he was 10 weeks old, he weighed about 50 pounds (22.7 kg). He was ready to start eating plants like his mother.

Baa, Baa, Mama!

A ewe is patient with her lambs—even when they climb on her to play "king of the hill"!

Chapter 2
A Sheep's Body

There are more than 200 kinds, or **breeds**, of sheep. Most have white or cream-colored wool. Some have wool that's two colors. Some have no wool at all!

Full of Wool

The most obvious part of a sheep's body is its woolly coat. Wool is fluffy and wavy, and helps keep sheep warm. It's a kind of hair, and it grows on other animals, such as camels, too. Wool is usually shorter than the stiff hairs that cover an animal's body. But most sheep grow wool that's longer than their stiff hairs.

Many kinds of sheep grow white or cream-colored wool, but sheep wool can also be black, gray, brown, or tan. Some sheep even have spotted coats! Some kinds of sheep also have faces and legs that are a different color from their body.

No Wool

Some kinds of sheep don't grow wool at all! They're called hair sheep. Farmers raise hair sheep in **habitats** with very hot weather, such as parts of Africa. These sheep provide milk and meat.

Hair sheep don't need wool to stay warm. If winter gets too cold, the sheep grow thick coats of hair to keep warm. In spring, they shed the extra hair.

Sheep Shapes

A sheep has a sturdy body and strong, thin legs. Each hoof is made up of two hard toes. A sheep has big ears that can turn in all directions, which helps the sheep hear sounds all around it. It can flare its nostrils to sniff the air for danger. Beneath the nostrils is a line, or split, in the sheep's upper lip. This split helps sheep pluck blades of grass to eat.

Sheep or Goat?

Some kinds of sheep look a lot like goats. You can tell sheep and goats apart by looking for a few clues. A male goat may have a beard. A ram does not. A goat has straight horns. A ram usually has curled horns. Many female goats have horns, but many ewes do not. A goat's tail is often flipped up, but a sheep's tail usually hangs down.

If you can't tell by looking, try using your other senses! A sheep's bleat sounds like "baa," while a goat's sounds like "maa." Goats also have a stronger odor than sheep.

Sheep look very different without their woolly coats!

People have found uses for rams' horns, which are hollow. One use involves producing sounds by blowing into them. In ancient times, people used rams' horns to communicate with others who lived several miles away.

Head of Horns

Many kinds of sheep grow horns. In some breeds, only the ram grows horns. In other breeds, both the ram and ewe have horns, but the ram's horns are bigger. Some breeds of sheep don't grow horns at all. They're called polled. A few kinds of sheep grow more than one pair of horns. Jacob sheep rams and ewes can grow four horns. Some even have six horns!

The outer layer of a sheep's horn is made of **keratin**. The inside layer is made of bone. People have long used sheep horns to make things, such as buttons and spoons. Horns are even used as instruments! Blowing into a hollow ram's horn makes a sound like a trumpet.

Sheep use their horns to protect themselves. Rams also use their horns to fight other rams. A ram's thick skull protects his head when he crashes his horns against another ram's head. The ram locks horns with the other ram and pushes and twists to knock him down.

Chapter 3

What Sheep Do

Sheep eat so much grass that the fields where they live don't need to be mowed.

Laze and Graze

Sheep spend much of the day eating. They graze on grass, weeds, and other plants in fields. A sheep has no upper front teeth. It has a rough pad on its gums instead. A sheep eats grass by pressing it between its lower front teeth and the pad. Then it tears the grass with a quick snap of its head. The sheep barely chews the grass before swallowing it. The food goes into two parts of its four-part stomach.

Later, the sheep coughs up a ball of grass called a cud. The sheep chews the cud with a side-to-side motion of its jaw. The cud is crushed and torn by the sheep's back teeth. Then the sheep swallows it again, and it goes to the other parts of its stomach, where it will be **digested**. Meanwhile, the sheep coughs up another cud to chew.

Sheep nip off plants very close to the ground. Farmers must be careful not to let sheep spoil a pasture by feeding in it for too long. Harming a pasture in this way is called overgrazing. Farmers also give sheep hay and grain to eat.

Sheep at Rest

The way sheep eat helps keep them safe from **predators**. Sheep quickly fill their stomach with grass when they're out in the open and then chew the food carefully when they're in a safe place. A sheep may spend hours chewing while it's lying down.

A sheep can sleep standing up, just as a horse can. But it sleeps more deeply when it's lying down. Baby sheep are full of energy. They run, climb, and play with other lambs. But, like young children, baby sheep lie down for naps.

On Guard

Sheep on a farm or ranch aren't safe from predators. Coyotes and stray dogs kill sheep and lambs. Bears and cougars sometimes eat sheep, too. Some sheep farmers use guard dogs to protect their sheep.

A guard dog doesn't herd sheep. Most of the time, the dog just hangs out with the sheep. It even sleeps with them. But it's alert for signs of danger. If a coyote comes near, the dog chases it away. Some farmers use llamas and donkeys to guard sheep. These animals call loudly if they see a predator. They may even kick the predator.

Every sheep in a flock knows its place. Some sheep act as leaders. The other sheep follow them to new grazing spots.

Ewe-nity!

Sheep are born with a strong need to be in a group, which is called a flock. A sheep gets nervous when it's alone. It bleats and paws the ground. This need to be in a group is called flocking behavior.

Flocking helps sheep survive. In a flock, many sets of eyes and ears are on guard against danger. If a predator appears, the sheep bunch together and run. The safest place to be is in the middle of the flock. There, a sheep is protected by the bodies of the other sheep. But even being on the edge of the flock is safer than being alone.

Flocking behavior helps people take care of sheep. A flock learns to follow the shepherd.

Sheepdogs

A herding dog, called a sheepdog, often helps the shepherd with the flock. Sheepdogs are born with the ability to herd other animals. A sheepdog runs around the flock to keep it moving. Even a hard stare from a sheepdog can get a flock moving!

Chapter 4
Wild Sheep

Heavy Horns

An old bighorn ram's horns can weigh up to 30 pounds (13.6 kg)—about as much as five newborn lambs!

Big-Horned Bighorns

Bighorn sheep live wild in western North America. Rams grow long, thick horns that curl. Ewes grow shorter horns. Bighorns graze in mountain meadows. Their hoofs have soft pads between the hard edges, which give bighorns a firm grip when climbing rocks. Bighorns never stray too far from the safety of cliffs.

Ewes and lambs form small herds for most of the year. Rams live separately. In fall, rams battle with each other for mates. In winter, ewes form bigger herds that may have up to 100 animals. An experienced ewe is the herd's leader.

Wolves, cougars, bears, bobcats, and coyotes hunt bighorns. Golden eagles sometimes snatch lambs. People also hunt bighorns.

Small Horns

Bighorn ewes grow shorter horns than rams do. A bighorn ewe usually has her first lamb when she's 2 years old.

Mountain Sheep

Dall sheep live on mountainsides in Alaska and parts of Canada. They're **nimble** climbers. Most Dall sheep are white. In a few locations, they're black or gray. Both rams and ewes grow horns. A ram's horns grow bigger and form curls, while a ewe's look like spikes.

Like bighorn sheep, Dall sheep form small herds. Ewes and lambs live together in spring and summer. In fall, rams join the herds. Rams charge toward each other and crash heads as they try to win mates. The sound of their horns smacking together can be heard a mile (1.6 km) away!

Dall sheep eat mainly grass and weeds in summer. In winter, they nibble on bushes and low-growing willow trees.

On the Rocks

Dall sheep can leap easily from rock to rock. This allows them to escape from predators who can't follow them up steep cliffs.

Barbary sheep are originally from North Africa. Today, they also live in Europe and the southwestern United States.

Wild but Not Woolly

A Barbary sheep's body is covered with hair the color of sand and stone. The hair is long and hangs from its throat like a beard. A ram's hair may grow all the way down to its front hoofs! A mane grows along the back of the Barbary sheep's neck. Barbary sheep are also called maned sheep. Both rams and ewes grow curved horns, but the ram's horns can be twice as long.

Barbary sheep first lived in northern Africa. The word "Barbary" comes from the Latin word *barbari*, which was the name used for the people living along the northern coast of Africa at the time of the Roman Empire. These people are known as Berbers today.

Barbary sheep live in mountainous deserts. Their sandy color helps them blend into their **environment**, making it harder for leopards and other predators to see them. Barbary sheep graze during cool mornings and evenings, and at night. By day, they rest in any shade they can find.

High Jumpers

Barbary sheep are great jumpers. From a stand-still position, they can leap over rocks 6 feet (1.8 m) high!

Chapter 5
Sheep and People

Have You Any Wool?

Sheep are best known for their wool. Wool is a very strong fiber used to make warm clothing. It's also used to make carpets, blankets, felt, baseballs, tennis balls, and other items.

A sheep's wool is removed by giving the sheep a hair cut, which is called shearing. Most sheep are sheared with a special kind of electric razor. An experienced shearer can shear a sheep in less than 2 minutes! The shearer cuts the wool so it comes off in one big piece, called fleece.

Sheep's wool contains a greasy, waxy substance called lanolin. Lanolin is used in soap and creamy lotions that make skin smooth and soft. It's also used as a **lubricant**.

More Sheep Products

Some breeds of sheep are raised for their milk. Sheep milk is used to make cheese, butter, yogurt, and ice cream. Other breeds are raised mainly for meat. Meat from a sheep less than 1 year old is called lamb. Meat from an older sheep is called mutton.

Different kinds of sheep grow different amounts of wool. Some very woolly breeds produce 30 pounds (13.6 kg) of wool per sheep!

Mouflons are wild sheep that live in parts of Europe. Although they don't look like the woolly sheep we're used to seeing today, mouflons are one of their **ancestors**.

Sheep History

People first began herding sheep about 7,000 years ago. Those sheep didn't look like modern farm sheep. They looked more like wild sheep, such as urials and mouflons. Urials still live in Asia, and mouflons live in Europe.

Ancient farmers favored sheep that were extra woolly or grew fat quickly. They bred these sheep to get lambs with these same qualities. Over time, breeding produced the different kinds of **domesticated** sheep that exist today.

Hundreds of sheep breeds are raised all over the world. China raises more sheep than any other country. Australia is the second-largest sheep producer. The third-largest is the island nation of New Zealand, which is home to about 39 million sheep. That's nine times more than the number of people in New Zealand!

Fast Facts About Farm Sheep

Scientific name	*Ovis aries*
Class	Mammals
Order	Artiodactyla
Size	Up to 4 feet (1.2 m) in length
Weight	Males from 150 to 350 pounds (68 to 159 kg)
	Females from 100 to 225 pounds (45 to 102 kg)
Life span	10 to 20 years
Habitat	Farms and ranches

Glossary

ancestor—a relative who lived long before you

breed—a specific variety of a type of animal. Also, to mate two animals with desired qualities in order to produce more like them.

digest—the body's process of converting food into usable substances

domesticated—bred and raised for use by people

environment—the conditions that surround a living thing and affect the way it lives

habitat—the natural environment where an animal or plant lives

keratin—a hard substance making up hair, fingernails, horns, and hoofs

lubricant—a slippery substance used to help parts slide easily over each other

nimble—quick and fast

nuzzle—to rub something gently or lovingly with the nose or face

predator—an animal that hunts and eats other animals

45

Sheep: Show What You Know

How much have you learned about sheep? Grab a piece of paper and a pencil and write your answers down.

1. Why do farmers dock sheep tails?

2. What kind of sheep can have four or six horns?

3. What are a sheep's horns made from?

4. How many parts does a sheep's stomach have?

5. How does flocking help sheep survive?

6. How do farmers keep sheep from overgrazing?

7. What type of wild sheep lives on mountainsides in Alaska and parts of Canada?

8. What is lanolin?

9. What is meat from an adult sheep called?

10. Which countries produce the most sheep?

1. To help keep sheep clean and stop flies from bothering them 2. Jacob sheep 3. The outer layer is keratin; the inside is bone 4. Four 5. Being in a flock is safer then being alone; if a predator appears, sheep bunch together and run 6. By giving them hay and grain to eat 7. Dall sheep 8. A greasy, waxy substance in wool used to make soap, lotions, and lubricants 9. Mutton 10. China, Australia, and New Zealand

For More Information

Books

Feinstein, Stephen. *The Bighorn Sheep: Help Save This Endangered Species!*
Berkeley Heights, NJ: MyReportLinks.com Books/Enslow Publishers, 2008.

Gandolfo, Flora. *Sheep*. Danbury, CT: Grolier, 2009.

Web Sites

American Sheep Industry Association: For Kids
www.sheepusa.org/for_kids
Read interesting facts about sheep, sheep farming, and wool.

Bighorn Sheep
www.defenders.org/wildlife_and_habitat/wildlife/bighorn_sheep.php#
Learn about bighorn sheep, their habitats, and what's being done to
protect them.

Index